Candor

The Unfolding Odyssey

Jhunel Wallace

Official King James Bible online. King James Bible Online.
(n.d.). https://www.kingjamesbibleonline.org/

Dedication

To those who lost their way from our Heavenly Father, He wants you to come home. To those who know of Him, but haven't established a relationship with Him, He wants you to know Him for yourselves. To those who have never met Him, He won't hesitate to welcome you with open arms.

Acknowledgments

God, I thank You for this amazing privilege. You allowed me to be a vessel in delivering what You spoke to me. Why You chose me, I'll never know. However, I am most grateful that You did. I will forever honor You Father, because without You none of this would be possible. Your presence was with me each day as I was putting my story into writing. On my own I would've never gotten this done in the timeframe in which it was completed. The orchestration of my story was done for Your glory, because You are worthy of receiving it. Everything that I am is a manifestation of Your matchless power. You took me on my first roller coaster, something I once told myself I would not venture on in real life. Even though it seemed scary, You helped me to overcome the fear that was within me and I knew in that moment, as I know now, how secure I truly am in You. Heavenly Father, You are my beginning and my end. All of this started with You and it will end with You.

Thank You, Father.

Contents

Chapter 1

Now I Can See

As we journey through life, it is not uncommon for us to lose sight of our true purpose and become fixated on worldly pleasures and pursuits. We may become so consumed with material possessions, power, and recognition that we forget to focus on the things that truly matter, and just like that, my focus, too, was on the wrong things.

It takes a moment of awakening, a moment of clarity, to realize that we have been walking down the wrong path. This realization can be jarring, and it may force us to confront uncomfortable truths about ourselves. It can be especially difficult to acknowledge when those truths involve our own egos and the ways in which we have been idolizing ourselves. I was so consumed to the point that I didn't even recognize that I was idolizing myself and I was living in sin without actual remorse.

When we idolize ourselves, we place our own desires and ambitions above all else. We become so focused on achieving our own goals and being recognized for our accomplishments that we lose sight of the bigger picture.

This kind of self-worship can lead us down a dangerous path, as we become blind to our own faults and shortcomings, and we fail to recognize the ways in which we may be hurting others. I never realized until this season of my life that I was headed down the wrong path.

Living in sin, as we have described it, is a symptom of this kind of self-idolization. My family, on many occasions, told me how vain I was, essentially having a great opinion of one's appearance or one's self altogether. I had to re-examine myself as God revealed the truth to me.

As we navigate through the complexities of life, it is easy to become fixated on our own egos and desires. We may become so consumed with our own image and accomplishments that we forget our true purpose and neglect the spiritual journey that we were meant to embark upon.

It is only when we are willing to confront the depths of our own vanity and self-worship that we can begin to awaken to the truth of our existence. For so long, I was blinded by my own ego, and my obsession with self-image had become a barrier to my spiritual growth. However, in a moment of divine grace, my eyes were finally opened to the error of my ways.

I came to realize that God had placed me on this earth for a higher purpose, one that was not centered on myself but rather on Him. I was put here to be a vessel for His light to shine through, to live in accordance with His scriptures, and to glorify Him in all that I do. Through His Word, God spoke to me and revealed the truth of my existence. It was in His delight that He made all things, and it was through Him that I would find my true purpose and fulfillment.

As I began to surrender my ego and turn towards God, I found a sense of peace and clarity that I had never experienced before. I learned that true spirituality is not about achieving perfection or attaining a higher status but rather about surrendering to the will of the Lord and aligning ourselves with His plan. According to Revelation 4:11, it reads, *"Thou art worthy, O Lord, to receive glory and honor and power: for thou hast created all things, and for thy pleasure, they are and were created."*

The yearning for a deeper connection with God is a common human experience. Many individuals have felt an emptiness within themselves, a void that cannot be filled by material possessions or worldly pleasures, and I was no different. It is a longing for something beyond ourselves, for something that transcends the limitations of the physical world.

In my quest for spiritual fulfillment, I searched for a word, a concept, or a belief that could provide me with a sense of purpose and direction. For some, it may be the acknowledgment of the Creator of Heaven and Earth, the Supreme Being. For others, it may be a different path, but the essence remains the same - a deep desire to connect with something greater than ourselves. I finally found the one that would acknowledge the Creator of Heaven and Earth. I knew that it was time to decrease so that God would increase. This was the beginning of my humble journey.

To embark on this journey requires humility - the willingness to decrease so that the Lord may increase within us. It is a recognition that we are but a small part of a vast and intricate creation and that our true purpose lies in serving a higher power. Yet, the world around us is full of distractions that pull us away from this path, and as I reflected on past events, the only description I had as it pertains to my previous self is that it felt like an illusion. It is easy to get caught up in the pursuit of power, money, fame, and success - all of which can bring temporary satisfaction but cannot fulfill the deeper longings of the soul. In fact, they often lead us further away from our spiritual center, creating a sense of disconnection and discontent.

The darkness of the world lurks in plain sight through the eyes of the spirit, and it is only by unlocking our inner vision that we can see beyond the illusion of materialism and embrace the truth of our existence. This vision is a gift from the Lord, and it can guide us toward a life of purpose and meaning. John 2:15-17, says,

> *Love not the world, neither the things that are in the world. If any man love the world, the love of the Father is not in him. For all that is in the world, the lust of the flesh, and the lust of the eyes, and the pride of life, is not of the Father, but is of the world. And the world passeth away, and the lust thereof: but he that doeth the will of God abideth forever.*

Throughout my journey, I have come to understand that the pursuit of material possessions and the temporary pleasures of this world only bring temporary satisfaction. It is only through a deep connection with a higher power that one can find true and lasting fulfillment.

As I have continued to seek a deeper spiritual bond with God, I have found that it is through the spirit that I am able to connect with Him. My prayers have been answered, and I have been blessed with a spiritual bond that allows me to navigate the uncertainties of life with faith and trust in God's plan for me.

For a long time, the struggle between the flesh and the spirit remained a constant battle. The desires of the flesh were overpowering and pulled me away from my spiritual path. However, through spiritual discipline and a deep commitment to following God, I have learned to overcome the desires of the flesh and align myself with the spirit.

This awakening has helped me realize that for most of my life, my flesh ruled my decisions and my actions. However, now is the time for my spirit to lead, and I am more than willing to follow. The realization that God's plans are far greater than my own has allowed me to let go of my previous desires to conform to societal standards and instead live a life guided by spiritual principles.

As a member of Gen Z, I understand the pressures to conform and do what is "cool" in the eyes of others. However, my spiritual awakening has taught me that true fulfillment and purpose can only be found through serving a higher power.

As I reflect on my past, I realize that there has always been a part of me that felt out of place in this world. I felt like I was constantly swimming against the tide, struggling to fit in and find my place. It wasn't until I fully embraced my faith that I came to understand why.

The world rejects God, and there is something inside of me that the world rejects as well - the presence of God in my life. This realization was a turning point for me. It allowed me to fully embrace my faith and accept that God's plan for me was different from the plans of the world.

Through the trials and tribulations that followed, I came to understand that God's plan was to separate me from the world, and He did just that. It was a new experience for me, but I decided never to look back, even if others chose to stay in the world.

This decision has not been easy, and it has included letting go of some of the dearest people in my life. However, I know that my family and friends have also met God, and He has a plan for all of us.

As I continue on this spiritual journey, I am reminded of the importance of serving God. It is through serving Him in spirit and in truth that I can fulfill my purpose and live a meaningful life. Despite the distractions that surround me, I remain focused on God and commit to following His path.

While the rejection of the world may have initially caused me pain and confusion, it has ultimately led me to a deeper understanding of my faith and my purpose. By embracing my spiritual path, I am able to serve God and make a positive impact on the world, even in the face of adversity.

> If the world hate you, ye know that it hated me before it hated you. If ye were of the world, the world would love his own: but because ye are not of the world, but I have chosen you out of the world, therefore the world hateth you. Remember the word that I said unto you, The servant is not greater than his lord. If they have persecuted me, they will also persecute you; if they have kept my saying, they will keep yours also. But all these things will they do unto you for my name's sake, because they know not him that sent me. If I had not come and spoken unto them, they had not had sin: but now they have no cloke for their sin. He that hateth me hateth my Father also. If I had not done among them the works which none other man did, they had not had sin: but now have

they both seen and hated both me and my Father. But this cometh to pass, that the word might be fulfilled that is written in their law, They hated me without a cause. (John 15:18-25)

Chapter 2

I Surrender

As I withdrew from nursing school, my heart felt shattered into a million pieces. I was utterly broken, with no hope of finding solace in this world. My soul was desperate for a change, a transformation that would heal me from the inside out. It was no longer enough to just dip my toe in the water; I needed to fully immerse myself in a new way of life. I was overwhelmed with a sense of conviction unlike anything I had ever experienced before.

I fell to the ground, tears streaming down my face, and cried out to God. "Please save me," I begged. "I can't do this on my own. I need You." The pain in my heart was indescribable, a weight that seemed impossible to bear. I wept day and night, lost in a sea of confusion and despair. My life felt meaningless, devoid of purpose.

But even in my darkest moments, I held onto a promise that God had made to me. I knew that He would never lie to me, and I clung to this hope with every fiber of my being. As I cried out to Him in my anguish, I felt a deep sense of peace wash over me. It was as if His love was wrapping itself around me, holding me close and reassuring me that I was not alone. Slowly but surely, I began to emerge from the darkness. I felt a renewed sense of purpose, unlike anything that I had ever experienced before. My spiritual awakening was not an easy journey, but it was one that ultimately brought me closer to God and to my true self. The scripture Jeremiah 29:11 are God's words of honor, "For I know the thoughts that I think toward you, saith the LORD, thoughts of peace, and not of evil, to give you an expected end".

I didn't have a clue about what was coming my way, but I sensed that it was no ordinary encounter when my Father took hold of me. As I stood there, I had an inkling that things were about to change, and for the better. The world had let me down too many times, and I had reached a point where nothing in it brought me any joy. I was disillusioned with the way things were, and I knew that there had to be more to life than what I was experiencing.

But then, in a moment of clarity, something shifted within me. It was as if a veil had been lifted from my eyes, and suddenly, I saw everything in a new light. The realization hit me with such force that I knew there was no going back. I was on a mission, and nothing would stand in my way. Despite my lowest moments, a voice spoke to me, reminding me that hope still existed and that all was not lost.

And so, I began to walk a new path, one that I knew would not be smooth but one that I was determined to take. With each step, I felt lighter, as if the weight of the world had been lifted from my shoulders. I embraced this newfound sense of purpose, and I knew that it would guide me to where I was meant to be. Though I couldn't see the road ahead, I trusted that God's grip would lead me to my destination. God's word from James 4:7-10 reads

> Submit yourselves therefore to God. Resist the
> devil, and he will flee from you. Draw nigh to God,
> and he will draw nigh to you. Cleanse your hands,
> ye sinners; and purify your hearts, ye double
> minded. Be afflicted, and mourn, and weep: let your
> laughter be turned to mourning, and your joy to
> heaviness. Humble yourselves in the sight of the
> Lord, and he shall lift you up.

As I surrendered myself to God's will, I felt a transformation taking place within me every passing day. Like a loving shepherd tending to his flock, God embraced me with open arms and watched over me. His grace and mercy were unlike anything I had ever experienced before, and their overwhelming power shattered my old ways, leaving them in ruins.

But this was not an instant process. Every day, God molded me like a skilled potter shaping his clay. The suffering I endured was a part of this refining process, and I knew I had to overcome it. I refused to let it break me down completely. There were moments when I felt so alone, and it was then that the enemy would try to take hold of me. But I refused to succumb to those feelings.

It was during one of those difficult days that I reached out to my sister in Christ. As I poured my heart out to her, she spoke softly and reassured me, "no, you are not alone. You are never alone." Her words touched me to the core, and tears streamed down my face. In the midst of my feeling of isolation, I realized that God was closer than I had ever imagined.

Through this journey, I learned to lean on God even in my darkest moments. I came to understand that even when I couldn't see Him, He was there, holding my hand, leading me down the path He had chosen for me. Each day, I grew more and more into the person He wanted me to be, leaving behind my old self and embracing the new creation He was making me into. And even in the midst of hardship and uncertainty, I knew that I was never truly alone, for my God was always by my side, "The Lord is nigh unto all them that call upon him, to all that call upon him in truth. He will fulfill the desire of them that fear him: he also will hear their cry, and will save them." (Psalms 145:18-19)

I have come to realize that the enemy has been deceiving me for far too long. His lies were like a veil that obscured my vision and led me astray. However, one day, the enemy attempted to stir up anger within me, but little did he know that God had already prepared me for this moment.

As I stood there, aware of the enemy's deception, I felt a wave of peace wash over me. It was like God was holding my hand, and I was no longer alone. At that moment, I understood that no matter how dire a situation may seem, God is always present, even when we cannot see or feel Him.

It was as though this was God's way of allowing me to prove my loyalty to Him. Although there may be times when He allows the enemy to fight us, it is only to make us stronger in our faith. Through it all, the Lord is waiting there, patiently, for us to put the enemy to shame.

As I laughed at the enemy and started thanking God for what He was doing within and around me, I could feel the joy within me begin to shine through. It was an indescribable feeling, and it was my time to testify.

Chapter 3

Behind the Scenes

When I committed to embarking on a profound spiritual journey with the Lord, I never could have fathomed the depths of transformation that awaited me. Yet, despite the enormity of the changes that transpired, my soul yearned for the glorious outcome that lay ahead. One day, a post online caught my eye, urging individuals to pray between the hours of 2:00 AM and 3:00 AM. It was as if a divine light illuminated my path, illuminating a clear course of action for me to take. In my naivety, I assumed that waking up at this hour would be a simple task, given my frequent bouts of insomnia.

However, I soon realized that the journey toward spiritual growth requires unwavering patience and unrelenting trust in God's divine plan. Gratefully, the benevolent hand of God guided me toward the right path, even when I was too weak to navigate it myself. Initially, I sought comfort and solace in my bed, yet I knew deep down that true prayer required a level of devotion and surrender that could only be achieved through deliberate action. So, with the strength of the Lord, I relinquished my physical comfort and humbly knelt upon my rug each night, dedicating myself to the pursuit of a deeper connection with Him.

After surrendering my shattered heart to God, my loved ones would inevitably inquire about my plans for the new year. As I shared the details of my spiritual journey, I could see the shock etched on their faces, their eyes widening in disbelief. Yet, to my delight, they began to ask me to pray for them, recognizing the transformative power of prayer. Through this sacred practice, I discovered an unwavering strength that flowed from the very essence of the Lord. The power of God's grace was made manifest in every moment of prayer, a testament to the Lord's eternal divine nature.

Whenever confusion clouded my mind, I turned to prayer as a way to seek clarity and direction, trusting that the answers would be revealed in God's perfect timing. In some instances, the response came quickly, and in others, it required steadfast patience and unwavering faith. Yet, through it all, I knew that God's hand was guiding me toward a greater understanding of the mysteries of the unseen world. I sought knowledge and wisdom through various mediums, from online sermons to ancient texts, knowing that my spirit and mind required the nourishment that only the Lord could provide.

In my journey towards healing, the Word of God served as my sustenance, providing the balm that my wounded soul so desperately needed, for I knew that the path towards spiritual wholeness required a holistic approach, one that recognized the interconnectedness of the body, mind, and spirit. Through prayer, I discovered a profound sense of peace and a renewed sense of hope, trusting in the divine plan that lay before me. Reading scriptures of healing allowed my faith in the Word of God to gradually increase, and my heart began to slowly mend. Psalms 147:3 says, "He healeth the broken in heart, and bindeth up their wounds."

Through my willingness to be vulnerable and open to the Lord, I discovered a deep sense of closeness and intimacy with God. As I confessed the brokenness that was within me, I felt the embrace of divine compassion, kindness, and love, filling me with a sense of peace, hope, and joy. The sanctuary of God's love became a refuge for my soul, offering a sense of comfort and safety that was not familiar to me. I longed to stay within this sacred space, shielded from the distractions and chaos of the outside world. And yet, even as I basked in the Lord's divine presence, I knew that there was still work to be done, that there were still lessons to be learned, and that there were still paths to be traversed.

One day, as I searched for a Bible online, I stumbled upon the realization that I already had one buried beneath a stack of books. In that moment of discovery, I felt a sense of relief and gratitude wash over me, knowing that the Lord had provided for my needs. Every detail of our lives is woven into the grand tapestry of the divine plan, a testament to the infinite wisdom and grace of God.

In a moment of recollection, I was reminded of a time at the Dollar Tree with my mother. It was the summer of last year, and we were shopping for items for my younger cousins. As usual, I made my way to the books section and stumbled upon a small, elegant Bible in white and gold. Without hesitation, I picked it up, feeling drawn to it. I didn't have a physical Bible at home, so I thought it was a sign to finally start reading the Word of God. I purchased it with the intention of diving into its pages, but unfortunately, it remained untouched in its plastic wrap for months. It was as if I had brought it home only to serve as a decorative piece on my chest of drawers.

However, as my spiritual journey progressed, I realized that God's timing is always perfect. The Bible had been waiting for me all along, and I knew I had to handle it with care and reverence. I prayed for God's guidance and wisdom as I delved deeper into the scriptures. My journal was always by my side, ready to capture my interpretations and insights. Whenever the enemy tried to attack me with negativity and lies, I wielded the sword of the Spirit to cut through the darkness.

Through this experience, I learned the importance of not only possessing the Word of God but also applying it to my life. The Bible is not just a book but a living, breathing entity that has the power to transform our hearts and minds. As I immersed myself in its teachings, I felt closer to God than ever before, and my faith grew stronger. Ephesians 6:16-18 says,

> Above all, taking the shield of faith, wherewith ye shall be able to quench all the fiery darts of the wicked. And take the helmet of salvation, and the sword of the Spirit, which is the word of God: Praying always with all prayer and supplication in the Spirit, and watching thereunto with all perseverance and supplication for all saints.

Previously, my mind was plagued by unpleasant thoughts that would take hold of me and leave me feeling powerless. Without the necessary resources, such as the strength of God, the discernment to distinguish truth from falsehood, the transformative power of prayer, the liberation of deliverance, the soothing balm of healing music, the wisdom of the Bible, and the purifying effects of fasting, I was at the mercy of my own mind. Fear and doubt had a stranglehold on me, and my decision-making was compromised by their insidious influence.

But as I began to cultivate a new mindset, one that was infused with spiritual depth and intensity, I felt a newfound power stirring deep within me. The once-dominant forces of fear and doubt began to lose their grip on me, and I was filled with a sense of spiritual confidence that surpassed anything I had ever known or experienced before. Even when these negative thoughts would try to take hold of me, I was able to dismiss them with ease.

Every morning, I would pray with a sense of authority that surprised even me. It was as if I was tapping into a power that was not my own but, rather, a divine force working through me. Through this experience, I came to understand the true might and power of God, and I was left in awe of the transformative potential of spiritual growth. This was not simply a matter of personal willpower or strength but rather a manifestation of the divine grace and love that flowed through me. Isaiah 41:10 says, "Fear thou not; for I am with thee: be not dismayed; for I am thy God: I will strengthen thee; yea, I will help thee; yea, I will uphold thee with the right hand of my righteousness".

My heart ached for the countless believers of Jesus Christ who were unaware of the wondrous spiritual journey that awaited them. I longed for those I knew and loved to experience the same profound connection with God that I had been blessed with. Yet, I understood that this was a personal journey that each individual must actively seek out and cultivate for themselves. As I delved deeper into my own spiritual journey, God began to reveal to me areas within myself that needed correction and healing. One of the most profound revelations came in the form of my own unforgiveness towards those who had hurt and abused me in the past.

For far too long, I had carried the weight of this pain and resentment within me, unable to let go of the hurt that these individuals had caused me. I realized that this unforgiveness was hindering my own growth and preventing me from experiencing the true freedom that God had in store for me. With God's guidance and grace, I was able to let go of the bitterness and resentment that had held me captive for so long.

In prayer, I poured out my heart to God, acknowledging the pain that these individuals had caused me and expressing my readiness to release it all. I also acknowledged my own imperfections and wrongdoings, asking for forgiveness and hoping that those I had hurt would extend the same grace to me. It was not an easy process, but the weight of the burden was far heavier than the thought of being forgiven. Forgiveness is a choice that only we can make, and it is up to us whether we want to remain stagnant or move forward toward the freedom that God has promised us.

As I delved deeper into the Bible, I came across a powerful scripture that resonated with me deeply. It spoke of how, when we refuse to forgive others, our Father in heaven will also refuse to forgive us as His children. This message served as a powerful reminder of the importance of forgiveness and the transformative power it can have in our lives. Through the grace of God, I was able to let go of my unforgiveness and experience the freedom and growth that came with it. Matthew 6: 14-15 says, "For if ye forgive men their trespasses, your heavenly Father will also forgive you: but if ye forgive not men their trespasses, neither will your Father forgive your trespasses".

As I immersed myself in the melodies of gospel music and worshiped God with all my heart, a sense of tranquility filled my very being. In those sacred moments, I felt the tangible presence of the Almighty, and my surroundings seemed to shift with a divine energy that left me with chills all over my body. Each time I lifted my voice in praise, a deep and abiding joy settled within me, and it lingered long after the music stopped. The magnitude of my love for Jesus intensified in ways I couldn't comprehend, and I was left in awe of the depth of our connection. It was unlike anything I had ever felt before, and my heart was bursting with a newfound fervor for Him.

Even though I had known about the sacrifice of Jesus for the sins of humanity, I now understood the full gravity of His actions. His selflessness and love had opened the doors of salvation for us, and I was filled with a deep appreciation for what He had done for me personally. John 15:9-14 reads,

> As the Father hath loved me, so have I loved you: continue ye in my love. If ye keep my

commandments, ye shall abide in my love; even as I have kept my Father's commandments, and abide in his love. These things have I spoken unto you, that my joy might remain in you, and that your joy might be full. This is my commandment, That ye love one another, as I have loved you. Greater love hath no man than this, that a man lay down his life for his friends. Ye are my friends, if ye do whatsoever I command you.

In moments of deep contemplation, I find myself pondering on the ultimate sacrifice that Jesus Christ made for humanity. It is a thought that fills me with awe and reverence and also prompts me to question my own faith and conviction. Would I have the courage to lay down my life for God if faced with such a choice? It is a question that tests the very core of our being and one that we must all ask ourselves.

Death is a reality that we all must face, but it is not something that should consume us with fear or anxiety. We are more than just our physical bodies, for we possess an eternal spirit that is sustained by righteousness. Only God holds power to destroy both body and soul, for it is He who created us. Matthew 10:28 says, "And fear not them which kill the body, but are not able to kill the soul: but rather fear him which is able to destroy both soul and body in hell".

Yet, in times of uncertainty and doubt, fear can often overshadow our faith and courage. We forget that our true selves lie within our spirit and that we are not defined by our physical limitations. We must remind ourselves to be bold and fearless in our trust and devotion to God, for He is the very embodiment of strength and courage.

Where God dwells, fear has no place. He is always with us, watching over us and protecting us from harm. Nothing can happen to us without His permission, for He is the ultimate authority and source of power. So let us walk in confidence and faith, knowing that we are never alone and that God is always with us. Lamentations 3:37 says, "Who is he that saith, and it cometh to pass, when the Lord commandeth it not".

As my relationship with Jesus grew deeper, it became apparent that the love I received from those around me paled in comparison to the love I received from Him. It was an unconditional, unwavering love that could only be experienced by those who truly know Him. This love was not something that could be manufactured or feigned, but it flowed naturally from my heart as a result of my experience with Jesus.

My hunger for Him grew stronger with each passing day, and I found that listening to worship music helped me to maintain my connection with Him. It was as though my soul was being nourished with spiritual food rather than physical sustenance. I was able to love because He first loved me, and this realization filled me with a deep sense of completeness. Colossians 2:10 says, "And ye are complete in him, which is the head of all principality and power."

As I continued to immerse myself in God's Word, my appetite for spiritual nourishment increased. Rather than being consumed by the desire for physical sustenance, I found myself craving a deeper connection with God. Meditating on His Word allowed me to reflect on the goodness of God in my life, and I was filled with a sense of gratitude and awe. Despite facing temptations to give up or lose focus, I remained steadfast in my commitment to God. Through this process, I discovered a new level of spiritual strength and even lost weight as my focus shifted from physical sustenance to spiritual nourishment.

As I contemplated the power of temptation and its hold over me, I came to realize that my thoughts and beliefs were integral to resisting its allure. With the help of God, I found the strength to overcome physical hunger and delve deeper into my spiritual connection with the Lord. Galatians 5:16 reminds us that living by the Spirit is the key to avoiding the pitfalls of the flesh, "This I say, then, Walk in the Spirit, and ye shall not fulfill the lust of the flesh."

In my quest for spiritual enlightenment, I came face to face with the concept of spiritual blindness. It was a daunting prospect, as I realized that being unaware of God's truth was a conscious choice that led to a lack of understanding. Only by turning to Jesus, the light of the world, could I hope to overcome my spiritual blindness and embrace the truth.

Yet, I also recognized that some people were so mired in their own perspectives that they refused to acknowledge the possibility of a higher truth. Their hearts were hardened, and they were unable to perceive the light of God. However, I remained hopeful, for I had experienced firsthand the transformative power of Jesus's healing touch. With Him by our side, we can open our eyes to the wonders of the Lord our God and embrace a life of love, truth, and spiritual fulfillment. 2 Corinthians 4:3-4 says, "But if our gospel be hid, it is hid to them that are lost: In whom the god of this world hath blinded the minds of them which believe not, lest the light of the glorious gospel of Christ, who is the image of God, should shine unto them".

Chapter 4
Under Construction

Being a seeker on a spiritual journey, I found solace and comfort in my daily routine of listening to music. However, I initially struggled to adapt solely to music that aligned with my spiritual beliefs and values. I would often listen to a wide variety of secular songs, which later brought on a great challenge for me to let go.

I soon realized that the music I listened to had a profound impact on my thoughts, emotions, and actions. I became mindful of the lyrics and messages behind the songs I sang along to. I questioned whether these messages were positive, whether they spoke to God, and whether they inspired me to lead a better life.

At a certain point, I came to the realization that the music I was consuming was not serving my spiritual growth. Some songs had a negative effect on my mood, causing me to dwell on past experiences and slowly leading me away from my spiritual path. I had to decide whether I wanted to be spirit led or led by fleshly desires. I began to lose my passion for secular music because it no longer resonated with me. Instead, I sought out music that touched my soul, lifted my spirit, and aligned with my spiritual beliefs. I found that by listening to music that nourished my soul, I was able to deepen my connection with God and experience a greater sense of peace and fulfillment. My heart was filled with joy, and the songs resonated deeply with my innermost being and kept me focused on the present moment.

As I delved deeper into my spiritual journey, I also became aware of the influence of movies on my life. I realized that just like music, movies could impact me emotionally, mentally, spiritually, and even physically. They could distract me from my spiritual path and keep me focused on the physical reality of the world. Many people get so caught up in the physical world that they forget or are unaware of the spiritual realm.

To open my heart and welcome God's presence into my life, I knew that I had to be in the right frame of mind and have my heart in the right place. I had to let go of the distractions and worldly pleasures that kept me from focusing on my spiritual journey. By doing so, I was able to give myself fully to God and receive His divine presence in my life. This allowed me to experience a deeper level of spiritual fulfillment and to live my life in a way that aligned with my spiritual beliefs and values, "Yet a time is coming and has now come when the true worshipers will worship the Father in the Spirit and in truth, for they are the kind of worshipers the Father seeks. God is spirit, and his worshipers must worship in the Spirit and in truth." (John 4:23-24)

One day, I was riding in an Uber on my way home, and the driver was playing gospel music, which filled my heart with joy and comfort. However, the genre suddenly shifted to hip-hop, which made me feel uneasy. So, I politely asked the driver if he could switch the music back to gospel music, which he kindly did. As we continued on our journey, he shared with me that he assumed I would prefer to listen to the latest secular music, given my age. While I understood his perspective, I couldn't help but feel that God was guiding me on a different path.

Reflecting back on my journey, I realized that just a few months earlier, I would have been content with listening to secular music. But now, my heart yearned for the spiritual messages in gospel music. I felt God's presence guiding me toward a more profound understanding of my spiritual path. At that moment, I prayed for strength to stay on the right path and to remain steadfast in my faith. I knew that the journey ahead would not be easy, but with God's fortification and guidance, I could overcome any obstacle.

Through this experience, I learned that even the smallest moments could have a profound impact on our spiritual journey. By staying attuned to God's presence and guidance, we can navigate through the challenges of life and remain on the path toward spiritual fulfillment, "Shew me thy ways, O LORD; teach me thy paths. Lead me in thy truth, and teach me: for thou art the God of my salvation; on thee do I wait all the day". (Psalms 25:4-5)

For several days, I immersed myself in contemplation of the fruits of the Spirit, reflecting deeply on their meaning and how they manifested in my life. I pondered whether the newfound love that had blossomed within me could withstand any obstacle and bring joy to my heart, whether peace reigned supreme in my life despite any challenges I faced, and whether I approached my struggles with patience and gentleness. I considered whether goodness was a habitual part of my character and whether my faith was deeply rooted in my heart. I also examined whether I maintained meekness in my thoughts and actions and whether I could overcome any temptation with temperance.

All of these reflections were aimed at evaluating my heart posture, ensuring that my interactions with others were guided by the fruits of the Spirit that had been cultivated within me. I yearned to share these fruits with anyone I came into contact with so that they, too, could experience the transformative power of God's love.

Through unwavering obedience to God, I have witnessed incredible signs, miracles, and wonders in my life. I have been blessed with love, joy, peace, patience, gentleness, goodness, faith, meekness, and temperance that I never knew existed. The ripening of these fruits has been a slow and steady process, spanning months. However, I now view the world through a lens of deep gratitude and a profound sense of awe at the progress that has been made within me through the grace of God, "But the fruit of the Spirit is love, joy, peace, forbearance, kindness, goodness, faithfulness, gentleness and self-control. Against such things there is no law."(Galatians 5:22-23)

Through the divine revelation of God's Word, I have been humbled and taught many valuable lessons about myself. In letting go of my ego and pride, I have found myself in a constant state of transition and growth, shedding old habits and behaviors that no longer serve me. As I reflect on my past mistakes and present shortcomings, I am able to acknowledge them with a heart of humility and a desire to improve. Though it may be difficult to admit fault and accept correction, I find solace in the fact that these moments of humility bring me closer to becoming the person God has called me to be.

In the face of correction, I find comfort in the knowledge that God always speaks the truth and corrects me out of a place of love. His Word is my guide, and I trust that His love will never lead me astray. For I have experienced the unfailing love of the Father time and time again, and in Him, I find a safe haven for my soul. Therefore, I surrender myself completely to His divine will, knowing that His plans for me are good and true. Through His guidance and correction, I continue to grow in wisdom, strength, and grace, becoming the person He has created me to be,"For whom the Lord loves He corrects, Just as a father the son in whom he delights". (Proverbs 3:12)

Letting go of ourselves and surrendering to God's will is an act of immense humility that requires great endurance. As we journey towards discovering our true identity as children of God, we must be prepared to stumble along the way, for the path is not always easy. The process of self-discovery involves accepting ourselves as God sees us, with all our strengths and weaknesses, and acknowledging that God's perception of us is not based on our physical appearance or what others say about us, but rather on the qualities of our spiritual being, "So God created man in his own image, in the image of God created he him; male and female created he them". (Genesis 1:27)

In our journey toward self-discovery, we must confront the fundamental question of who we truly are. Are we defined by our mistakes, our thoughts, or the opinions of others? As we grapple with these questions, we must remind ourselves that we are God's children, saved by grace through faith and fashioned in His image. We are His beloved works of art, and He loves and forgives us unconditionally.

This realization is not dependent on anything we can do on our own or anything anyone else can do for us. It is solely based on our relationship with Christ and who we are in Him. Through His grace, we have been welcomed into God's family, and this humbles us beyond words. As we reflect on our journey, we must remember that it is an honor to be taken from the depths of our struggles and be embraced by the love of Christ. We are grateful for His constant presence in our lives, guiding us toward our true identity and purpose.

> O LORD, thou hast searched me, and known me. Thou knowest my downsitting and mine uprising, thou understandest my thought afar off. Thou compassest my path and my lying down, and art acquainted with all my ways. For there is not a word in my tongue, but, lo, O LORD, thou knowest it altogether. Thou hast beset me behind and before, and laid thine hand upon me. Such knowledge is too wonderful for me; it is high, I cannot attain unto it. (Psalms 139:1-6)

As I embarked on a journey of self-discovery and embraced my purpose and identity in Christ, I sought guidance from the Lord to understand how I could best serve Him. Writing a book had always been a dream of mine, but it never made it to the top of my priority list. However, one day, during a divine encounter, God spoke to me and told me to start writing. My cousin Kelsey had suggested that I document my daily experiences, but I had always brushed it off with the excuse of not having enough time. But now, God was urging me to share my story with others, and I could not turn a deaf ear to His call.

Initially, I thought that every moment spent away from writing was a wasted opportunity. However, God had other plans for me. He wanted me to rest my mind for a few days each week, and I began to feel guilty for what I believed was procrastination. But I soon realized that taking breaks was essential for me as a new writer, as it prevented me from becoming overwhelmed. Sometimes, events that occurred in my life would trigger my creativity, and other times; my mind would draw a blank. I struggled with a range of mixed emotions that threatened to derail my progress. However, I reminded myself that God was in control, and I needed to trust His timing.

Rather than rushing through the writing process, I began to slow down and appreciate the time I spent cultivating my story. I realized that by being patient and creative, I would produce a better outcome. Through this process, I gained a deeper understanding of my purpose and discovered the spiritual value of slowing down to find my truth. By surrendering my fears and doubts to God, I found the inspiration and motivation to share my journey with the world, "Before I formed thee in the belly I knew thee; and before thou camest forth out of the womb I sanctified thee, and I ordained thee a prophet unto the nations". (Jeremiah 1:5)

During a phone call with my cousin Tedra, we discussed our daily lives and caught up on what we've been up to. As we neared the end of our conversation, Tedra remarked, "You've changed." I was taken aback and asked her to explain. She said, "Your personality it's been imbued with holiness." I chuckled and asked her to slow down. But she insisted it was true and expressed her desire to be like that too. Her words brought a smile to my face, and I responded, "I feel different. God is doing something." Tedra agreed, "I can tell."

However, I confided in her that it hadn't been an easy journey. There were nights when I cried out to God, questioning why He was changing me. It wasn't that I didn't want the change, but it was overwhelming at times. Despite the challenges, I knew that God was doing something extraordinary in my life, and I was grateful for it.

Hearing Tedra say that I had changed made my heart skip a beat. I was nervous about the impression it might give her, but I also wanted to encourage her that change is possible for anyone who seeks Jesus. We all have moments when we yearn for a different view of life and a deeper connection with Christ. That burning desire to follow Jesus and witness the transformation in others is a powerful force that only God can ignite.

When God works in our lives, the change is ongoing and continuous. Our spirits expand and unfold, revealing more of our true selves. It's not just about becoming a better person, but it's about becoming the person God created us to be. As we allow God to shape and mold us, we become vessels of holiness, radiating His light to the world around us.

"Wherefore comfort, yourselves together, and edify one another, even as also ye do."

1 Thessalonians 5:11

Chapter 5

The Waiting Period

In the midst of a deeply transformative phase, I found myself confronted with a monumental challenge. It was a time when my faith and patience were being refined in the crucible of life. As the new day dawned, I applied for a job I believed I had longed for in vain. In my ignorance, I neglected to seek divine guidance in this decision, unaware that the Almighty's wisdom should permeate every aspect of my existence, even my career choices.

When the organization's silence left me in limbo, I turned to prayer, beseeching the Creator for clarity on whether I should pursue alternative opportunities. His enigmatic response revealed that I was, in fact, already engaged in meaningful work. Puzzled, I inquired further, only to be gently reminded that the writing project I had embarked upon was a divinely appointed task.

The notion of multitasking flitted through my consciousness, but how could I dare to question the Lord's divine plan? Humbly, I acknowledged my role as a servant of the Most High, resolving to focus solely on the writing He had entrusted to me. At that moment, I relinquished my need for understanding, choosing instead to place unwavering trust in God.

With my heart resolute and my path illuminated, I followed the sacred guidance, confident that this time, my patience would not be in vain. I embraced the journey ahead, knowing that every step taken in faith would bring me closer to the fulfillment of my spiritual purpose, "Wait on the Lord: be of good courage, and he shall strengthen thine heart: wait, I say, on the Lord". (Psalm 27:14)

As I journeyed through life, I discovered that relying solely on my own understanding was akin to crossing a perilous path. The human mind, limited in its capacity, could never truly grasp the full magnitude of the Lord's omnipotence. God's wisdom is unparalleled, transcending our mortal comprehension.

The eternal struggle between the desires of the flesh and the guidance of the spirit pervades every aspect of our lives, even when deciding upon a career or a job. Many of us, myself included, often overlook the importance of seeking divine counsel in these matters. Left unchecked, the cravings of the flesh can easily overpower our minds, leading us down a self-centered path.

To overcome this inclination, we must diligently train ourselves to submit our fleshly desires to the authority of the spirit. As fallible beings, we must continually remind ourselves to remain steadfast, brave, and hopeful. Mental strength and moral strength are essential in our quest to conquer the temptations of the flesh.

We must remember that we are not our own; we belong to a higher power. As such, our lives should not be dedicated to the pursuit of self-interest but rather to the divine purpose that has been bestowed upon us, "For whether we live, we live unto the Lord; and whether we die, we die unto the Lord: whether we live therefore, or die, we are the Lord's". (Romans 14:8)

In the silence of midnight, as I immersed myself in divine communion with the Almighty, I boldly proclaimed the nature of my forthcoming day. Miraculously, the vision I cast invariably manifested itself, even amidst the commotion of life's challenges. I grasped that I was not the sole orchestrator of my destiny but rather an instrument in the grand symphony of existence.

Truly, the power of life and death resides in the spoken word, as we are called to continually breathe life into our being and weave a tapestry of blessings in our daily encounters. In the past, I remained unaware of the profound effect of the words that poured from my lips and unwittingly sowed toxic seeds in my soul.

The sacred wisdom that all spoken words wield the power of creation or destruction, regardless of the intent behind them, illumined my consciousness. I grasped that words could only nurture or wither, uplift or subdue. As I embraced this revelation, I cultivated the habit of speaking tenderly to myself, and in turn, my interactions with others filled with newfound grace.

With avid conviction, I declared my days to be blessed, wondrous, exuberant, miraculous, awe-inspiring, and resplendent. I became a vessel for peace, love, and luminous light. Our words carry an ethereal weight, bearing the capacity to elevate us to great heights or cast us into the abyss. Let us choose wisely, for in our words lies the power to shape our very existence, "Death and life are in the power of the tongue: and they that love it shall eat the fruit thereof". (Proverbs 18:21)

In the divine presence of the Creator, our manner of speech toward and about others is never concealed. God's omniscient gaze penetrates our outward facades, discerning the essence of our hearts, whether our words spring from the wells of benevolence or malice. He perceives the sincerity or deception veiled behind seemingly innocent jests and feigned guilelessness.

As children of the Most High God, we are guided to uplift one another rather than tear each other asunder. Yet, all too often, our actions belie the wisdom we profess. Embarking on a path of speaking goodness and light into the lives of others does not occur in the blink of an eye. For some, it demands perseverance and conscious effort. As followers of Christ, we recognize that belittling others will never serve our spiritual growth.

Our words are mirrors, reflecting the inner landscapes of our souls. Thus, we must exercise vigilance in our speech, for when we sow discordance instead of offering assistance, we unwittingly unleash a storm upon our own lives. Conversely, when we extend a word of encouragement to a fellow seeker, we create blessings that flow back to us.

However, let us not be driven by self-interest in our acts of kindness. Instead, let our motivation spring from a deep love for Jesus and an unwavering desire to emulate His compassionate example. In doing so, we foster a world imbued with love, empathy, and spiritual resonance, "A good man out of the good treasure of his heart bringeth forth that which is good; and an evil man out of the evil treasure of his heart bringeth forth that which is evil: for of the abundance of the heart his mouth speaketh". (Luke 6:45)

Embracing the Lord's divine plan and relinquishing our own desires opens the door to complete reliance on the Almighty. In surrendering our will, we kindle within ourselves a yearning for the path He has laid before us. To walk in the footsteps of Jesus is to shed our former selves daily, casting aside the shackles of old habits and patterns. We may be unable to see just what our future looks like, but as God is an understanding God, enthroned on high and looks low, He sees and knows everything.

This is the authority that only He holds. On our own, we are very limited in what we can do. But the presence of God in our lives pushes that limit beyond anything. It is rather good to be quick to follow God's plan than our own.

In the ever-present dance between heaven and earth, we must ultimately choose whom we serve, for time waits for no one. Each of our journeys is on a unique and divinely ordained timeline, known only to God, whose loving guidance is available to all who invite Him to illuminate their way.

Though our mortal vision is obscured, unable to discern the unfolding of our destiny, God's all-seeing wisdom perceives the tapestry of our lives from a spiritual point. In our inherent limitations, we can only achieve so much, but when we invite the presence of the Lord into our lives, we transcend the boundaries of earthly constraint.

Choosing to follow God's plan swiftly and wholeheartedly ensures that we are continually showered with His blessings. As we embark on this spiritual journey, we may grapple with doubts about our ability to submit to God's divine will or concern ourselves with the opinions of those around us. Yet, even in the face of opposition or solitude, choosing to dwell in communion with God is all that truly matters.

The children of God need not fear the ill intentions of others, for He assures us that divine justice will prevail. The truth is our Creator already knows the choices we will make. The question remains: do you? "No weapon that is formed against thee shall prosper; and every tongue that shall rise against thee in judgment thou shalt condemn. This is the heritage of the servants of the LORD, and their righteousness is of me, saith the LORD." (Isaiah 54:17)

As the cold evening air enveloped me, I found solace on my rug, preparing to immerse myself in the divine wisdom of a sermon on my phone. A shiver ran down my spine, urging me to seek the warmth of my cherished blanket. As I enveloped myself in its cozy embrace, the blanket's gentle motion inadvertently toppled my phone stand.

It had never occurred to me to use the stand, but at that moment, a quiet whisper in my soul suggested its usefulness. I felt as if the Lord was guiding me to utilize the stand, allowing me to view the sermon with ease, sparing my neck from the strain that had previously caused discomfort. To some, this may seem trivial, but within the depths of my connection with the Lord, I recognized His tender care.

The profound relationship I share with the Creator has taught me to cherish every act of grace, no matter how seemingly small. For in the intimate presence of God, we find ourselves in a sacred space of prayer and anticipation, awaiting the revelation of what lies beyond the breakthrough. Our hearts race with eagerness, pondering when the fulfillment of His promise will be unveiled – minutes, days, or even years from now.

Yet our human nature often leads us to doubt, making it difficult to place our unwavering trust in the Lord. Perhaps it is fear of the unknown that steers our minds toward uncertainty, or maybe the presence of doubt allows God to demonstrate the miraculous. We are each unique in our faith, some harboring more doubt than others, but through our spiritual journey, we come to recognize the boundless love and support of our Creator.

Witnessing the unwavering faith of others can serve as a powerful reagent, inspiring us to embrace our own journey of spiritual growth. When we align our hearts and minds with the Divine Word and foster an intimate relationship with the Creator, we come to understand that His blessings are reserved for us, awaiting our acceptance. The choice is ours: to embrace His promises, knowing they will never be unfulfilled, or to dismiss the possibilities laid before us. The omnipresent gaze of the Lord watches over each of our steps, accompanying us in every moment of our lives – in our quiet prayers, our daily routines, and even in our moments of silent contemplation. Isaiah 55:11 reminds us of the potency of God's word:

"So shall my word be that goeth forth out of my mouth: it shall not return unto me void, but it shall accomplish that which I please, and it shall prosper in the thing whereto I sent it".

Indeed, the Creator's unwavering support is a constant for His children, even when others may fail us. Our existence is devoid of true meaning without a connection to the Lord. All too often, we become entangled in the world's expectations and lose sight of our spiritual purpose. It is crucial that we break free from the confines of societal norms and remember that we arrived in this world with nothing, and we will depart in the same manner. Earthly possessions and achievements will ultimately fade, but salvation through Christ offers eternal hope and solace.

Embracing the realization that the world is fleeting and impermanent can liberate us to focus on our spiritual growth and deepen our relationship with God, the only true and everlasting source of fulfillment.

I have seen all the works that are done under the sun; and, behold, all is vanity and vexation of spirit.

Ecclesiastes 1:14

Chapter 6

Total Transformation

The divine love of the Almighty rescued me from the depths of darkness. For a long time, I had resisted His call, thinking I was not yet prepared for the profound transformation that comes with embracing Christ's teachings. It's natural to feel hesitant and unsure about submitting oneself fully to the will of the Lord. But it is through our openness and willingness to accept Jesus that our spiritual journey begins.

Many are called, but few choose to follow the path laid out by God. We often get caught up in our own desires and fail to realize that our lives are not ours to control. We must surrender our will to the Lord and be willing to make sacrifices in order to prioritize God in every aspect of our lives. It's not just during our toughest moments that we should turn to Him, but also in our moments of triumph and joy.

When we commit to walking with God, He will always be present in our lives. His love and grace will guide us through even the darkest of days. We must trust in His plan and know that His light will always shine upon us, for it is through His love that we are saved, and it is through our unwavering faith in Him that we can truly experience the wonders of the spiritual journey.

The Lord, in His infinite wisdom, chose to love and accept me despite my past sins. It's a humbling realization that the Lord sees past our faults and loves us unconditionally. As we deepen our relationship with Him, we unlock a greater understanding of our spiritual selves and open ourselves up to the boundless dimensions of His kingdom. It's an exciting journey of growth and enlightenment.

In this spiritual journey, God reveals different aspects of Himself to us through dreams and visions. These are sacred moments of communication between ourselves and the Lord, where He imparts knowledge and insights that may not be immediately discernible. It's like reading the Bible, where sometimes we need to interpret the message before it becomes clear to us. Similarly, with dreams and visions, we need to seek the interpretation and guidance of the Holy Spirit.

Sometimes, we may wake up from a dream feeling confused or unsure of its meaning. But this is where our trust in God comes in. By asking Him to help us understand the message behind the dream, we open ourselves up to His divine wisdom and insight. However, we must also be discerning and recognize that some dreams may be influenced by our own thoughts and desires. It's crucial to seek clarity and confirmation through prayer and meditation.

Through dreams and visions, we deepen our spiritual connection with God and gain a greater understanding of His will for our lives. It's a beautiful and awe-inspiring journey of faith and discovery, and we are blessed to have a loving God who chooses to reveal Himself to us in such profound ways, "And it shall come to pass in the last days, saith God, I will pour out of my Spirit upon all flesh: and your sons and your daughters shall prophesy, and your young men shall see visions, and your old men shall dream dreams" .(Acts 2:17)

God, the divine Creator of the universe, is ever-present and always ready to move in our personal lives. He desires to transform our old ways of living and thinking that don't align with His will and bring forth something new and beautiful. He sees us when we are struggling and in need of saving, but we must humbly cry out to Him and invite Him into our hearts.

When we set aside our pride and allow ourselves to be vulnerable before God, He pours out His goodness upon us. He longs to fill our hearts with His love, grace, and mercy, but He needs us to be receptive and open to receive His blessings. I can testify from personal experience how good God has been to me throughout my spiritual journey of change, "And be not conformed to this world, but be ye transformed by the renewing of your mind, that ye may prove what is that good, and acceptable, and perfect, will of God". (Romans 12:2)

I remember a time when I prayed for healing for my aunt's friend when I was young, and God answered my prayer. This experience planted a seed of faith within me that has continued to grow and blossom over the years. Recently, as I have delved deeper into my relationship with God, I have come to understand that prayer is a powerful tool for connecting with Him and experiencing His presence.

Through the ups and downs of life, I have learned that God is always faithful and present, ready to help me overcome any obstacle. Looking back at my past circumstances, I can see how God's blessings have been woven throughout my life. My heart is filled with gratitude for the strength and guidance God has provided, allowing me to persevere and continue my journey. Without God, none of it would have been possible, and I am humbled and grateful for His constant presence in my life, "For by grace are ye saved through faith; and that not of yourselves: it is the gift of God:Not of works, lest any man should boast. For we are his workmanship, created in Christ Jesus unto good works, which God hath before ordained that we should walk in them". (Ephesians 2: 8-10)

We will experience a joy beyond our understanding that can only be found in God. This is a joy that surpasses all earthly pleasures and possessions, and it is available to everyone who seeks it with a sincere heart.

God's grace is not dependent on our possessions or accomplishments. It is freely given to us because of who He is, not because of what we have done or what we own. We cannot buy our way into heaven, but we can enter through the narrow gate of salvation by accepting Jesus as our Lord and Savior.

> And seeing the multitudes, he went up into a
> mountain: and when he was set, his disciples came
> unto him: And he opened his mouth, and taught
> them, saying, Blessed are the poor in spirit: for

theirs is the kingdom of heaven. Blessed are they that mourn: for they shall be comforted. Blessed are the meek: for they shall inherit the earth. Blessed are they which do hunger and thirst after righteousness: for they shall be filled. Blessed are the merciful: for they shall obtain mercy. Blessed are the pure in heart: for they shall see God. Blessed are the peacemakers: for they shall be called the children of God. Blessed are they which are persecuted for righteousness' sake: for theirs is the kingdom of heaven. Blessed are ye, when men shall revile you, and persecute you, and shall say all manner of evil against you falsely, for my sake. Rejoice, and be exceeding glad: for great is your reward in heaven: for so persecuted they the prophets which were before you. (Matthew 5:1-12)

When we surrender our lives to God and abide in His truth, we find security in knowing that our eternity is secure in Him. This assurance comes from living a life that is Christlike, where our thoughts, words, and actions are in alignment with His will. It requires acknowledging our sins and turning away from them in repentance, with the confidence that we are forgiven and favored by God.

As we embark on this journey of faith, we can trust that God will guide us every step of the way. He understands our unique situations and knows what areas of our lives need to change first. By embracing the uncomfortable and making changes that align with His word, we can experience the joy and fulfillment that comes from living a life that is pleasing to God. So let us choose the path of life and continually pursue Christ, for in Him, we will find the true meaning of our existence.

> That ye put off concerning the former conversation the old man, which is corrupt according to the deceitful lusts; And be renewed in the spirit of your mind; And that ye put on the new man, which after God is created in righteousness and true holiness. (Ephesians 4:22-24)

As I reflect on the boundless grace and immeasurable mercy of the Lord, my heart is filled with gratitude for the path that has led me to this moment. Through each twist and turn, every triumph and trial, my capacity to receive divine teachings and guidance has expanded, illuminating every aspect of my journey and every area in which I have grown.

As I abide in the presence of God, meditating on sacred scriptures day and night, I am reminded of the sovereignty of the Lord's will and the faithfulness of the Lord's guidance. Though the path before me may be fraught with challenges and obstacles, I remain steadfast in my trust that God's plan will prevail and nothing can veer me off course.

Through the complexities of this journey, I have not lost sight of the power of faith in action. Through Christ's example, I have learned that faith without works is empty, and I have been emboldened to persevere through every trial with unwavering faith and steadfast determination.

This spiritual awakening has brought a refreshing breeze to my soul, soothing the weary places within and bringing a sense of wholeness and healing that can only come from the Lord. I stand renewed, ready to continue on this journey with a heart full of gratitude and a spirit fortified by the Lord's grace and mercy.

Oh, the sweet liberation that comes from shedding the cloak of pretense and living in the truth of who we were created to be! No longer do we seek to blend in with the world, for we have embraced our identities as beloved children of the Lord. Growing up in church alongside my siblings and cousins, we were all familiar with the concept of God's existence. I fondly recall attending Wednesday services with my sister Leah and how our youthful hearts were filled with wonder and awe.

Along my spiritual journey, I have often reflected on the moment when Leah encountered the Holy Spirit. As she knelt at the altar with tears streaming down her face, I saw a transformation in her that had remained etched in my mind. Her encounter with the Lord emboldened me and strengthened my faith that God can do for my family what He has done for me on this sacred path.

In hindsight, I can see how the hardships I faced along this journey have deepened my appreciation for the blessings of this path. It may seem impossible, but it is true - my struggles have gifted me with an awareness of the Lord's unwavering grace and mercy that sustains me through every trial.

Through this journey, I have felt a renewed sense of urgency to share with others the transformative power of God's grace. I am humbled by the opportunity to bear witness to the wonders of this journey and to guide others toward the light of the Lord's infinite love and mercy.

As I reflect on my journey thus far, I am filled with a deep sense of gratitude for the unwavering presence of God in my life. Through every trial and tribulation, He has been my constant companion, guiding me through the ups and downs with unrelenting love and compassion. It is in those moments of solitude, where it's just me and God, that I truly feel His embrace and am able to fully comprehend the depth of His grace.

For those seeking a deeper connection with a higher power, I implore you to look no further than God. While we may interact with others throughout our lives, ultimately, it is our relationship with God that sustains us through the trials and tribulations of life. In those moments of quiet contemplation, we are able to experience the transformative power of His love and discover that there truly is no other like Him.

In my own life, I have experienced firsthand the miraculous power of God to bring beauty from ashes. When I was in the midst of heartbreak and suffering, it was God who held me close and comforted me with His unyielding love. He stripped away everything that was not essential and, in doing so, revealed to me the true depth of His mercy and grace.

As I journey forward, I hold fast to the knowledge that God never changes. In a world that is constantly shifting and evolving, His love remains steadfast and true. He is the only one who can rescue us from any and everything, and it is only through Him that we can find true peace and fulfillment.

In my journey of spirituality, I have come to understand that God's divine plan surpasses my limited human comprehension. He had allowed every event, every joy, every pain, and every struggle in my life to unfold exactly as it did, knowing the outcome before it even happened. At times, I thought that certain things were the most important to me, only to realize that they were fleeting and temporary. But through it all, I have grown to appreciate that God is the ultimate source of my being and my purpose.

As I surrendered my life to God, I began to witness a transformation within myself. It wasn't the people around me who were changing; it was me. And as I underwent this metamorphosis, my perception of the world around me began to shift. What once seemed mundane and ordinary now appeared in a new light, as if I was seeing everything for the first time.

Now, as I look back on the journey I've been on, I am reminded of the immense love and grace that God has shown me. I am being released from the unfolding of my past and stepping into a future that is filled with endless possibilities. Yet, I know that my spiritual journey is far from over. It is only just beginning as I continue to deepen my relationship with the Almighty and discover new truths about myself and the world around me.

Being confident of this very thing, that he which hath begun a good work in you will perform it until the day of Jesus Christ.

Philippians 1:6

Chapter 7

Let's Pray

As I stood before Jesus, I felt a powerful wave of emotion wash over me. At that moment, my eyes were opened to a level of clarity I had never experienced before. I saw Him in all His perfection and glory, and I knew that I had never truly understood what true perfection looked like until now.

As I gazed upon Him, I couldn't help but notice the stark contrast between His perfection and my own imperfection. It was as if a veil had been lifted from my eyes, and I could finally see myself for who I truly was - a flawed and sinful human being.

Through my encounter with Jesus, I came to understand that my previous way of life was not in line with God's will for me. I saw how I had been living in opposition to His Word, seeking to please myself rather than to serve Him.

But in His infinite mercy, God opened the eyes of my heart so that I could see the truth that had been right in front of me all along. I realized that the enemy had been diverting my attention away from the truth, leading me down a path of sin and destruction, "And immediately there fell from his eyes as it had been scales: and he received sight forthwith, and arose, and was baptized". (Acts 9:18)

As I found myself grappling with the weight of my personal affairs, I felt as though hope was slipping through my fingers like sand. It was a dark and lonely place, with nowhere to turn and no one to turn to. But then, in my darkest hour, I heard a still, small voice calling out to me. It was the voice of Jesus, reaching out to me with open arms, beckoning me to turn to Him.

In my confusion, I had been making plans for my future for all the wrong reasons. But through my encounter with Jesus, I came to understand that He had a plan for me, one that was far greater than anything I could have imagined for myself.

Through His guidance and His love, I began to unearth the desires that were buried deep within my heart - desires that aligned perfectly with His will for me. I realized that my dreams and aspirations should be placed in God's care and that only He could lead me down the path He had designed for me.

It was not an easy journey, but I learned to surrender all that concerned me to God's loving care. I gave Him my hopes, my fears, my doubts - everything that I thought defined me - so that He could purify me into the person He had called me to be.

And so, through my struggles and my surrender, I emerged stronger, more fully connected to God, and more confident in the knowledge that His plans for me were perfect in every way.

In the depths of our being, a battle rages on, a conflict between light and darkness, a struggle for our soul's destiny. The forces of evil relentlessly try to thwart our path and hinder us from realizing our purpose on this earthly plane. The adversary cunningly seeks to blind us to our true identity, shrouding our vision with a thick veil of confusion and doubt.

But the truth is that we are created in the image of God, and our destiny is to fulfill a unique purpose that only we can accomplish. Once we awaken to this realization, we are empowered to overcome any obstacle, and the darkness of our past can no longer hold us back. For when we see ourselves as God sees us, we become unstoppable, an unstoppable force of love, peace, and grace.

The enemy knows this, and he will stop at nothing to keep us in bondage, to prevent us from claiming our rightful place as children of the Most High. Even when we turn away from our rebellious ways, he still persists, trying to lure us back into old patterns of behavior, attempting to drag us down into the abyss of despair and defeat.

But we must not give up; we must not surrender to his deceptions. For we are not alone in this battle, and we have the power of God within us. Let us hold fast to our faith, let us stand firm in our convictions, and let us boldly declare our identity as children of God. For in doing so, we will emerge victorious, and the enemy will be defeated.

> All that the Father giveth me shall come to me; and him that cometh to me I will in no wise cast out. For I came down from heaven, not to do mine own will, but the will of him that sent me. And this is the Father's will which hath sent me, that of all which he hath given me I should lose nothing, but should raise it up again at the last day. And this is the will of him that sent me, that every one which seeth the Son, and believeth on him, may have everlasting life: and I will raise him up at the last day.

> (John 6:37-40)

In life, we are called to grow and change, to become more like the God-image that we were created to reflect. God begins this transformation by working within us, constructing a new character that is aligned with His will. This process requires us to let go of our old ways of thinking and behaving and embrace a new identity in Christ. It is a process that requires adjustment as we shift our focus from ourselves to God.

To help us in this journey, we must immerse ourselves in God's word and allow the Holy Spirit to guide us in our refinement. We must learn to take delight in every experience, even the challenging ones, for it is through these experiences that we grow and mature in our faith.

As we journey through life, we must sow seeds of positivity and goodness, for it is only through these actions that we can hope to create a more positive and loving world. The enemy seeks to undermine our progress by tempting us to complain and grumble, but we must not give in to his tactics. We must remember that we are called to a higher purpose and that our ultimate destiny lies in the hands of our Heavenly Father, "My people are destroyed for lack of knowledge: because thou hast rejected knowledge, I will also reject thee, that thou shalt be no priest to me: seeing thou hast forgotten the law of thy God, I will also forget thy children". (Hosea 4:6)

We are often tested by the challenges that come our way. It is in these moments of trial that we must strive to maintain the right attitude toward God. When we find ourselves growing weary and impatient while waiting for our deepest desires to be fulfilled, we must pause and take a moment to reflect on our inner selves.

Through prayer and contemplation, we can attain a deeper understanding of our true purpose in alignment with the will of God. The enemy is cunning, and without the wisdom to recognize his deceptions, we may fall into his trap and act impulsively, moving without the guidance of God.

Yet, we must not be discouraged. For even in our most trying moments, a connection with God can bring us the assurance we need to persevere. We must not forget that our breakthrough may be just around the corner, and yielding to the enemy's schemes can be a grave mistake.

It is essential to remember that God's timeline is not the same as our own, and so we must trust in God's plan and timing. When we rely on God, victory is inevitable, and our desires will be fulfilled in due time. However, if we try to forge ahead in our own strength, we risk falling into defeat,

"And he said unto me, My grace is sufficient for thee: for my strength is made perfect in weakness. Most gladly therefore will I rather glory in my infirmities, that the power of Christ may rest upon me". (2 Corinthians 12:9)

As we pause to reflect on our journey, we come to realize the profound impact that receiving Christ into our lives has had on us. Before that moment, we were lost souls, our hearts encased in stone, unable to fully embrace our Savior. We may have been blinded to the love of God, but it was always there, waiting for us to open our hearts and receive it.

Despite our past mistakes and the many times we may have strayed from the path of righteousness, God has always been there, offering us the chance to turn away from our sinful ways and find redemption. It takes courage to step into the person we were truly meant to be and to allow our spirits to be led by a vision that is centered on Christ.

In the past, we may have been swept away by the currents of the world, lost in a sea of confusion and uncertainty. But through the grace of God, we have emerged on the other side, stronger and more resolute in our faith. We have found clarity amidst the chaos, and our journey is now focused on one path, one destination: our Heavenly Father.

As we walk this path, we are filled with a sense of purpose and fulfillment that can only come from a life dedicated to serving God. We are no longer slaves to our past, but instead, we have been set free to live a life of true meaning and significance. With each step we take, we draw closer to God, and our hearts overflow with gratitude for the love and mercy that he has shown us.

> Charity suffereth long, and is kind; charity envieth not; charity vaunteth not itself, is not puffed up, Doth not behave itself unseemly, seeketh not her own, is not easily provoked, thinketh no evil; Rejoiceth not in iniquity, but rejoiceth in the truth; Beareth all things, believeth all things, hopeth all things, endureth all things. (1 Corinthians 13:4-7)

As we submit ourselves to God's presence within and around us, we are called to embark on a journey of self-discovery and spiritual awakening. With open hearts and minds, we invite God to probe the depths of our souls to reveal our true essence and purpose. In this quest for enlightenment, we must remain steadfast in our devotion, prayerful, and mindful of God's guidance that surrounds us.

Every aspect of our lives should be imbued with the wisdom and grace of the Almighty, and His word should be our compass, leading us toward the path of righteousness and salvation. As we commune with God in prayer, we should not only focus on our own needs and desires but also extend our love and compassion to all those around us.

Our prayers should encompass not only our loved ones but also those who have crossed our paths, both known and unknown, for every soul is a precious creation of God. As we offer our heartfelt supplications, we become vessels of His grace, spreading His light and love to all corners of the world.

Whether we choose to pray for individuals or for the collective, our deeds on earth should be driven by our faith and devotion. For there is no greater reward than to hear the voice of the King of Kings and Lord of Lords, proclaiming, "Well done, my faithful servant."

> I exhort therefore, that, first of all, supplications, prayers, intercessions, and giving of thanks, be made for all men; For kings, and for all that are in authority; that we may lead a quiet and peaceable life in all godliness and honesty. For this is good and acceptable in the sight of God our Saviour;

Who will have all men to be saved, and to come unto the knowledge of the truth. For there is one God, and one mediator between God and men, the man Christ Jesus; Who gave himself a ransom for all, to be testified in due time. (1 Timothy 2:1-6)